Even Now You Lead Me

WRITTEN BY
DONNA SINGLETON

Donna Singleton

Copyright 2018 by Donna Singleton. No part of this book may be used in any form or by any means graphical, electronic, or mechanical without written permission of the copyright owner.

ISBN: 978-1-987852-12-7

First printing January 2018

Author: Donna Singleton; 340 Cape Bear Road;
Murray River Box 2; Murray River, PE C0A 1W0; Canada

Publisher: Wood Island Prints; 670 Trans-Canada Highway, RR1; Belle River, PE C0A 1B0; Canada;
(902) 962-3335; schultz@pei.sympatico.ca; www.woodislandsprints.com

Printer: Lightning Source Inc. (US); 1246 Heil Quaker Blvd, La Vergne, TN 37086; USA;
(615) 213-5815; inquiry@lightning-source.com; www.lightningsource.com

Additional copies of this book may be obtained from the author or the publisher

I DEDICATE THIS
TO ALL MY CHILDREN,
GRANDCHILDREN, FAMILY,
FRIENDS AND ALL WHO CAN
BENEFIT IN ANY WAY
FROM LIFE'S EXPERIENCES
AND MY VIEW ON LIFE'S LESSONS.

Even Now You Lead Me

EVEN NOW, YOU LEAD ME is based on life events up to age sixteen of a young girl from Prince Edward Island. She hopes this will relate with people of all ages. Her wish is that this book will give some encouraging and helpful advice to families and their loved ones. The picture on the title page is of the author, Donna Singleton remarrying the love of her life Ronnie Singleton joined by her five children, grandchildren, daughter-in-law and son-in-laws. After thirty-eight years of marriage, her children and family organized, arranged, and financed the dream wedding she had always wanted. With great pride she would like to dedicate this book to her children, family and friends.

Donna Singleton

Table of Contents

1: Ellen's Trust and Innocence is Taken 1

2: Childhood Faith 5

3: Just wanting to be a Child 6

4: Pre-Teen Crushes versus Reality 8

5: Still Hoping for Trust 10

6: Ellen Prays for Change 12

7: A Fathers Betrayal 13

8: Ellen Speaks Out for Her Mother and Herself 14

9: Ellen's Time in High School 16

10: Summer Fun and Adventure 17

11: Ellen Meets Darcy 20

12: A Difficult Time for Ellen 22

13: Ellen Reluctantly Forgives 27

14: Helena and Ellen go Dancing 33

15: No Dream Date for Ellen 42

16: Quiet Times and Just Being Happy 45

17: Ellen's Meet's Farren 47

18: Ellen's Date 48

19: Why did he not keep their date? 51

20: After Farren 54

21: Ellen's First Funeral 55

22: Dougie's Wake 56

23: Ellen Meets Terry 58

24: Ellen's Letter and Prayer 60

25: Reflections 62

26: Conclusion Stories 63

27: New Beginnings 70

1: Ellen's Trust and Innocence is Taken

As they drove up to the farm, Ellen asked Frank if there were little yellow chickens in the barn.

"I sure hope so, Ellen—we'll see in a minute, won't we?" as Frank stopped the car in front of the barn.

Ellen was about six years old at the time of this story.

Ellen's dad's friend Frank was visiting one hot summer day. Mom had asked Dad to go to the neighbour's farm for eggs and milk.

Frank offered to go, "Come on Ellen, do you want to go see the chickens?"

She giggled as she ran to the car yelling to Mom, "Be right back Mommy, we're going to see the chickens."

Andrea came running after her, yelling at the top of her little lungs, "I want to see the chickens too."

"Can Andrea come too?" Ellen asked tugging on Frank's jacket.

"Come on then, get in the car, Andrea." in an irritated tone.

As they drove up to the farm Ellen asked if there were little yellow chickens in the barn.

"I sure hope so Ellen, we'll see in a minute won't we?" He stopped the car in front of the barn.

"Can I go see the chickens too, Frank?" Andrea chanted.

"One at a time, Andrea, maybe when we come out. You stay here and Frank will get you a treat." as he helped Ellen out of the car.

Ellen looked back at Andrea and waved to her, thinking it must be too much trouble to take both of them in.

"We'll just go right in and see the chickens Ellen. Let's hurry." as he led her to the barn door.

Don't we have to ask the farmer first for our eggs and milk?" Ellen did not see the farmer.

"It's alright. The farmer is in the field; he'll be here soon."

"Ok, I guess," as Frank took her hand and they headed into where the chickens, and cows were in the barn.

Frank continued holding her hand and led her to a corner, "Where's the little yellow chickens, Frank?" as she nervously looked around.

"There just over there, Ellen, but first I want you to let me check something." Frank said in an authoritative tone.

"What do you need to check?" she said innocently looking at Frank, thinking there must be something wrong with her.

"Well, this won't hurt and if you are a good girl, I'll give you a nice chocolate bar as a reward." Frank sounded just like a doctor.

She didn't think he was going to hurt her so she just stood there and said," Then can we go see the little yellow chickens Frank?"

"Of course we can Ellen, now come here and let Frank check you," as he carefully lifted her dress and with his fingers he pushed hard into her.

He then released Ellen and straightened her dress as he patted her head and took her by the hand again. He told her, "You were a very good girl and everything is fine Ellen. We can go see the chickens now.

"Then I'll get the eggs and milk, and that chocolate bar that I promised you. *Now you mustn't tell anyone about me checking you, or you won't get that chocolate bar."*

"Alright Ellen, this is our secret isn't it?" Frank spoke a little sterner this time than before.

She didn't want him to know she was scared and that checking hurt her. She tried desperately not to cry and, still standing there with her head down so as not to see his face, just nodded in agreement and politely said, "I don't want to see the little chickens now, Frank. Can we go now?"

"Sure, Ellen, we can see them later if you want. You get in the car, and I'll get the milk and eggs." He stated in a tone as if everything was fine.

Again she just nodded and got in the car and sat there confused not having a clue what this man had just done to her or why.

Andrea, thinking it was her turn to see the chickens, opened the car door yelling to Frank that it was her turn, only to be picked up and thrown back in the car as he yelled, "We don't have time to see the chickens now, Andrea. Your Mom is waiting for the eggs and milk."

Andrea turned her face to Ellen, tears running down her cheeks and softly whispered, "I want to go home Ellen! Frank is a bad man."

Ellen tried not to let Andrea see she was scared as she told her, "Frank will take us home when he brings Mommy's milk and eggs."

"Ok, Ellen. I don't like Frank no more." in between sniffles and soft whimpers.

"I know. It'll be ok, Andrea."

Frank came back with the milk and eggs, "You alright, Ellen? Your chocolate bar *I promised you for keeping our secret* is in the dash." He reached over, opened the dash, and placed the bar in her hands.

All she could do was nod *yes* and sit there as Frank took them home.

At home Frank carried in the eggs and milk and put them on the counter saying,

"Ellen was a great help getting the eggs and milk and we saw the little yellow chicks. Wasn't that fun Ellen, we'll go again another time won't we?"

Frank was looking at her as she said, "Ok, I guess so."

All she wanted right then was to hide in her attic room and never come out.

She excused herself saying, "Mommy, I'm going to play with Suzie," and ran to her room as quickly as she could.

She cried quietly, trying not to let her Mom hear her. That checking did hurt, and she didn't know why Frank hurt her or why it was a secret. He said not to tell, so she couldn't.

She had to go to the bathroom, that's when she discovered she was bleeding where Frank checked her. She was terrified she was dying.

Her Mom did hear her crying, though. Ellen doesn't remember what she said—just that she couldn't tell her secret to her Mom.

Mom had seen that she was bleeding and asked her what happened. Just what Mom said she doesn't remember, except that she couldn't tell her secret to her Mom. She doesn't know why and feels she never will. What she does know is *that man left her with a fear of being alone with or trusting men*.

Ellen always wondered why she never felt she could really confide in her mother as she should have been able to. Her mother never as far as she could remember talked to her about important things a girl should know.

Doreen through all her years of marriage to Donald, depended on him to take her wherever they needed to go. Shopping was somewhat supervised and on a time schedule as he was untrusting of her. She faithfully stayed by his side despite all his shortcomings. She was always a quiet woman as far as sharing her life stories with her children.

2: Childhood Faith

Ellen, a feisty, little freckle faced redhead has believed in *Christ* ever since she can remember. So with a tender trusting heart and a zest for knowledge, six-year-old Ellen began her journey.

Ellen's faith became deeper and stronger as she was introduced to Sunday School by her neighbours. She has always been thankful to them for bringing her with them. Her little white catechism book gave her pride and enthusiasm to learn more about *Christ as* she memorized the verses and enjoyed the fellowship. She felt as if she belonged—that there really was someone looking after her. She learned that if she needed help with anything, she could turn to *Him*. Ellen was grateful for the opportunity and lessons she learned. Just knowing that *Christ* will never leave her was such a blessing.

I here relate Ellen's story—based on true-life events—with children, teens, and parents in mind. Bringing awareness of sexual abuse and how the abusers are usually people we know and trust is her prayer. Children are trusting and easy targets for sexual predators, especially if the predator is known to the victim.

Ellen's prayers each night always include loved ones, friends, family, and people from around the world. She hopes by sharing her mistakes and bad experiences she can help someone avoid going through some similar situations.

3: Just wanting to be a Child

Ellen grew up finding it hard to trust the men in her life. She didn't trust the man her Dad worked for—the way he looked at Ellen made her nervous. But he never made any advances. She remembers saying back then that she would never marry anyone with his last name. Guess what? She did.

When she was about nine, these things started happening again. Her dad's friends and her uncle made Ellen uncomfortable when they visited. She was walking in their lane one day. Her uncle, who she knew had been drinking, asked, "Give old Uncle George a hug, Ellen."

Thinking she was going to just give him a quick hug, Uncle George instead squeezed her real tight. She could feel him touching her in a bad way, so she pushed him away as hard as she could and ran to the house. Again she felt she shouldn't tell anyone and felt dirty. She became more confused than ever about how to react to men.

Ellen's favourite companion next to Andrea was her Suzie doll, given to Ellen for Christmas by her first Grade teacher, Mary Ross.

Content to sit in her attic bedroom with Andrea and her Suzie doll, she would gather some old clothes, needle, thread and scissors and whip up a new wardrobe for Suzie while listening to the radio.

One time she thought that Suzie needed a handbag. It would have to be real fancy—maybe brown alligator would be nice. She asked Andrea if she thought Dad would mind if she took a little piece of his old guitar case to make Suzie a nice purse since he wasn't using it anyway. Ellen giggled as Andrea put her hands on her hips and pouted that she wouldn't help—it would make Dad mad.

"No he won't Andrea, it's just an old guitar case, come on, help me please." Ellen pleaded, knowing she would help her.

"Ok Ellen, but Daddy will get mad." Andrea said as she picked up the neck end of the old guitar case, giggling as they carried their project of to her room.

The purse turned out pretty good, and, to cover their tracks, they dragged the old case back to its corner in the attic.

Their Dad was none the wiser until quite a few years later when Ellen confessed what she'd done. Ellen was sure Mom and Dad must have noticed Suzie's fancy brown leather alligator bag, for when she asked her Dad if he was mad at her, he said simply, "It was just an old case. It's fine dear; I didn't need that old thing anyway."

Ellen's dad, Donald, was a well-liked hard-working man all his life. He worked many hard labour jobs, including at a lumber camp in New Brunswick on Lumpston's Mountain. Ellen learned to walk up there. Her Mom gave her a copy of a picture of several couples posing outside the camp including her holding Ellen with her Dad.

Her Dad played in a band back then. He was a great fiddler. Back on the Island, he worked cutting pulp wood and later in the gravel pit, where he picked up the nickname Fred Flintstone. He also worked in the tobacco fields.

For many years, he played fiddle, guitar, banjo, accordion, and harmonica—practically anything playable he could play. He was a good singer as well, similar to Hank Williams. He played at many places including Legions and house parties.

But her Dad had a problem—he drank—heavily and often. He was a good worker, but as he became an alcoholic, he was no longer very nice to his family. Many times he would come home and accuse her mom of foolish things that existed only in his head. She didn't think he was physically abusive to her Mom, but verbally he was terrible. Her Dad's friends were drinkers as well, and she hated it—they all made her nervous, and she hated being around them. Her Dad was a jealous man, but he didn't practice what he preached. Despite all his shortcomings, they all loved their Dad and always would. He had fallen victim to a terrible disease, alcoholism, and they all paid the price.

4: Pre-Teen Crushes versus Reality

As Ellen neared her teens and became aware of boys she had some serious crushes—never people she knew personally. She would see a guy on television and was sure it was love. Her first crushes were the stars of *The Man from U.N.C.L.E.* namely *Napoleon Solo* and *Ilya Kuryakin*. They were so dreamy!

By the time the program came on at night, she and Andrea were supposed to be in bed. They weren't allowed to watch TV that late. But there was an opening in the ceiling below her attic bedroom that was conveniently over the TV. They would lie on their bellies peering through the hole, watching as their heroes always caught the bad guys and they usually fell asleep dreaming about Napoleon and Ilya—the latter specifically Ellen's hero.

In Ellen's dream world the perfect man would be such a gentleman. He'd treat her like she was a princess, and would always lead her out on to the dance floor, bow to her as he takes her hand and lead her in such a beautiful waltz, that would be the envy of everyone in the room. After their waltz the gentleman would take her gently in his arms and kiss her. She would feel as though she would melt in his arms and their love would be pure and endless.

(Reality). For the time being, she was content to continue her celebrity crushes.

When he wasn't drinking, her Dad was a wonderful person, and she loved him very much. She was learning, though, that even her Dad could change into someone she could not trust.

She knew alcohol has the ability to turn a good person into someone you would not even recognize. It becomes a nightmare for the people who love them. Why do they do the things they do? Why are they so mad and suspicious of everyone? Maybe when they can't trust their own actions, they don't trust anyone else either.

Ellen's life became a constant struggle to avoid any situation that would leave her alone with her father or his friends. If she knew there was a chance of being alone, she would keep her little sister Andrea close by.

Her father would go out drinking with his friends and come back a couple of days later, furious with her Mom. Maybe this was his way of shifting the blame away from himself. She always knew there was no truth in his accusations, but in *his* head, he believed it. The next day he'd sober up and be himself again and wouldn't even remember what he'd said or done.

For a time, he stayed sober and Ellen began trusting him again. She was so happy to have her Dad again. Then he said he would teach her to drive, and she was overjoyed.

They began by practicing backing up and parking in their yard. It was fun except she backed up one day into the guide wire on the light pole leaving a scrape the length of the car. She got scolded a bit, but it was nothing serious, and she soon forgot about it. Those times were a good memory for Ellen—her dad was sober, and she felt she was able to trust him.

5: Still Hoping for Trust

When Ellen was thirteen, her Mom was nearing her due date for the arrival of their new baby sister or brother.

Aunt Louise, (who was actually their cousin), would be helping with the laundry, dishes, and meals during the day and would be taking care of them all while Mom was in the hospital. Ellen's Mom's oldest sister is Louise's mother. The children always thought she was an *aunt* because she was so much older. She had three children of her own, but she was always happy to come help them out, leaving her husband, Wilbur, home with the kids.

Ellen felt *she* could look after the house and make the meals without any help from Aunt Louise, and resented how overly friendly she seemed with her Dad—especially with poor Mom going to the hospital to have a new baby. But since her father had started drinking again, making Ellen nervous to be around him, she tolerated Aunt Louise's visits.

One evening they needed something at the store and Dad said, "Ellen, let's go to the store for Mom. You can drive to the end of the gate."

"Can Andrea come too, Dad?"

"Andrea you wait here with Mom; we'll be right back."

Ellen was reluctant but she thought if he hadn't been drinking nothing would happen. And driving to the end of the gate would be fun.

She drove to the end of the lane, and then he drove to the store. On the way back, he stopped and asked Ellen to *do something for him* and said it would make him feel better.

At thirteen she had no idea why this would help him feel better as she said, "Is that enough, can we go home now Dad?"

"Alright Ellen, you want to drive in the lane?" He said as if everything was perfectly normal.

"That's ok Dad, I'm tired and we have school in the morning," just wanting to go home—she'd know better the next time.

They arrived home, and she hurriedly gave Mom a kiss goodnight and headed to her room.

Little sister Andrea came to her room a little later and asked, "Ellen can I sleep with you, please?"

Ellen knew Andrea could sense when she was upset, and of course she welcomed her company. Without her little sister she would have become just a shell of a person. Andrea had become a shelter from the unwelcome advances of men, and the bond they share is with them to this day. Andrea, is four years younger and has always been her best friend.

6: Ellen Prays for Change

The day arrived for their mother to go to the hospital to have the baby. After mother went to the hospital, father began drinking quite heavily again. Prayer was Ellen's only escape—talking to the Lord reassured her she wasn't alone.

So she prayed ...

Dear Lord:

I don't know what to do anymore, Dear Lord. Please help me. All I can do is cry and try to stay out of his way. Please make Dad stop drinking and be our father again. I'm so afraid to be in the same room alone with him or any other guys for that matter. Why do guys want to do these things to me? Is this all men want? What do I do? Please show me how I should be and make me a good girl, Dear Lord. I will do as You ask.

Thank you Lord. Amen.

Ellen knew the *Lord* answers prayers in *His* time. "*He* will not put us through anything we cannot bear" she thought. "There must be a reason my sisters and I go through these things." To Ellen, knowing this made them stronger and more understanding.

She could not have the courage to tell you of these experiences if she hadn't truly gone through them herself and come out the other side. With that in mind, it makes it easier to tell you, with the hope that you may avoid these awful things from happening to you or to someone you know.

7: A Fathers Betrayal

With her Dad drinking every day once her Mom went to the hospital, Ellen reluctantly tolerated Aunt Louise. She suspected her Aunt was more than friends with her Dad, but let it pass in the hope of being left alone. Aunt Louise stayed with the family, cleaning, cooking, and doing the laundry, which was fine.

The day before Ellen's Mom was due to come home with their new sister (Melinda), Aunt Louise went home, and that evening Dad was still drinking.

Andrea and Ellen stayed up late watching television until they were really sleepy. They waited to see if Dad would fall asleep in the old chair so they could creep up to bed. When he started snoring with his head tilted back and mouth open they climbed up their attic ladder to bed.

Andrea fell fast asleep so Ellen read herself a story to help fall asleep. She dozed off, only to be wakened by her father dragging her to the stairs by her hair. He was very drunk and she couldn't understand what he was saying to her. All she knew was she was scared and didn't know what was going to happen to her.

He still had her by the hair when he threw her onto his bed. He mumbled something like, she was beautiful, and climbed on top of her. She can't explain it but thinks, as best she can remember, he never actually went all the way—the rest is a blur.

She has long tried to blot this out of her memory like it happened to someone else, so it makes it easier for her to tell you. An experience such as this leaves a child forever changed. Some girls may hide the truth forever, not telling a soul for fear of what the consequences would be. It can be swept under the rug or their truths can be brought to the surface in writings such as this. For generations it has been mostly unspoken and hidden. Ellen's life's secrets would have remained just that if not for the power of written words, giving us the power to express our worst fears, or our complete joy, through faith. He gives us these choices and ability to tell our story. Whether happy or sad, tell your story!

8: Ellen Speaks Out for Her Mother and Herself

On one fateful day at age fourteen, Ellen decided to stand up for herself and her Mom. Her father had been gone for a couple of days on another binge. He came bursting in the front door ranting and raving about some imaginary man behind the stove that her Mom was supposedly hiding from him.

Ellen could not take it anymore and exploded, screaming at him, "That's enough Dad! You know Mom isn't doing anything—you are. You've been gone for two days and you come home here yelling at Mom. You leave my Mom alone and leave me alone too! We don't know you anymore, Dad. I don't want to live here like this. This is not normal. I hate living here!"

Ellen was still waving her arms and yelling when he just sat down not saying a word and hung his head, and began to cry.

Ellen couldn't bring herself to console him, nor did her mother. All his days her mother would never talk back to father. Ellen assumed she was afraid of him, but she did truly love him. His serious drinking problem had become a way of life that they had begun to think was normal.

When you have a loved one that has an addiction of any kind, you learn to tip-toe around your home. When the addicted person is at home, you tippy toe, especially when they fall asleep, for fear they will awake and be angry with anyone that gets in their way.

After Ellen intervened with her father—assuming that's what we'll call the blow up—Ellen felt more at ease at home. It wasn't long before he was drinking again, but he avoided her, and she was relieved to be able to feel safe.

She started hanging out with her cousin Helena, swimming, dancing, and just talking. They were like sisters and had a ball together. It never occurred to Ellen at any time that her sisters might be at risk at home, but they were.

Her sister Joyce hated having her hair brushed for school each morning. She would sit on her chair, crying, as Ellen brushed her tangled golden brown hair. It was no surprise when she missed the bus from all her fussing.

To settle some of Joyce's morning fussing over her hair being so tangly, Ellen decided to cut it, which she did. It helped little Joyce with her morning tangles.

She had no knowledge that they were experiencing the same abuse she had gone through. She only discovered this just last year when she asked Andrea if she would give her opinion on her writing. Andrea read what she had written up to that point and, with some tears, told Ellen it was well written *and true*. Andrea was finally free to confide in her sister, telling her she went through similar experiences.

Ellen felt like she had abandoned her younger sister back then. Andrea reassured Ellen it wasn't her fault—like Ellen, she felt she had to keep those bad things to herself.

About that same time Joyce, through her poetry, was able to release some of the burden she held within herself for all the years of abuse she endured. Joyce is seven years younger, than Ellen.

It is a shock to realize that all three girls were going through these traumatic experiences at such a young age and no one seemed to know.

9: Ellen's Time in High School

About the time Ellen started high school she and her family had to move to an old farm house in the country while renovations were made to their home. She was now becoming aware that the boys in school were noticing her. They would occasionally ask if she would like to play a game of tennis. She could not bring herself to say *yes* and would shy away. She enjoyed the attention but didn't want it to go any further.

Ellen loved school and studied hard, aiming for the best marks possible. If she failed at anything she considered herself a failure and she wanted to prove she wasn't.

When she turned fifteen, she would be officially allowed to date. Still, she was not interested in anyone that way. Crushes were fine—*they wouldn't hurt you*. All the other girls were dating and Ellen would overhear them laughing and sharing their secrets. All through grades nine and ten Ellen avoided guys, and they seemed to avoid her.

She passed grade ten and intended to return for grade eleven, but money was scarce, and she never returned. This is one of her lifelong regrets—not finishing school. Her life seemed unfulfilled—night after night she'd have a dream where she was in school trying to find her home room and awake before she did. If it were up to Ellen, every child would have the opportunity to have every advantage possible to get their education.

Ellen would like to pass on to all you young people, this bit of advice, "If there's anything you might learn from my experiences I would hope this would be one of them—please don't give up on your education. It is one of your most valuable assets. Enjoy it while you're young. Take advantage of every opportunity out there and make your life worthwhile. Believe in yourself. It is so hard to get an education after you drop out of school. So if you're lucky enough to have an opportunity to finish your education, just do it!"

10: Summer Fun and Adventure

Ellen's only brother, Leroy, was born two years and one month after her.

Leroy was quite the boy—there was the time when he took her Suzie doll and slit her mouth open and inserted a big bottle. Over the years Ellen tried different methods to mend poor Suzie's mouth including stitching it with a needle and thread and gluing it with *Lepages* glue (which wasn't such a great idea).

Memories of Leroy as they got older were full of adventures together. Just walking home from school with Leroy, Andrea, and Stewart (a friend in her School class), would find them all kinds of adventures. There was nothing they enjoyed more than investigating abandoned farmhouses. Unlimited treasures and adventure might be just around the corner when they entered those once-bustling homes.

One afternoon the four of them were heading for the shortcut home through the cattle path, they got side-tracked by an old farm house. The excitement of what would be found lying around or tucked away in a hidden treasure box—perhaps in the attic—was just too much to resist.

Ellen and Andrea scuffled through old papers and dusty old pieces of plaster that fell from the walls. Ellen found a big old portrait of Abraham Lincoln, or so she thought, and showed the boys.

Over in the corner the boys found a gallon of robin egg blue paint, and the art work began. They covered that lovely painting with huge clops and smears of chalky blue and threw some of the plaster dust on for special effect, and then headed up the stairs for some more adventure.

Stewart hoisted Ellen up to the attic door as Leroy steadied him. She pushed the attic door open and peered around, putting her hand on a small red figure she carefully grasped, thinking it would be a nice gift for Mom. As she handed it down to Stewart they heard footsteps and a loud voice downstairs. They quickly helped Ellen down and grabbed Andrea's hand as they scurried to a door-less closet and hid. Shivering in fear, Ellen clutched her newly found little red treasure—a crossed-legged man with a turban on his head.

"What are young rascals doing up there? It's dangerous in this old house! Get on home before I give you all a licking," the man roared.

They stood shivering in that closet, terrified that the man was going to shoot them. The footsteps were getting louder as the man came up the stairs, and suddenly they could see him with his back to them as he said in that loud voice, "You kids better be getting down them there stairs before I turn around or you'll be all getting that lickin' I promised! Now get."

They wasted no time running down the stairs and down the cow path with their hearts pounding, not daring to look back.

Stewart's house came first, so they saw him home and he went up his lane laughing, saying, "See you guys tomorrow; we won't take the shortcut tomorrow, but maybe we can check out that old house behind the apple orchard at the end of our road, ok guys?"

Leroy looks at Ellen and laughs saying, "Sure thing Stewart; we'll see you at school."

Years later Ellen learned the figure was a Buddha, but no matter; Mom liked it just fine.

The Landing was an inlet from the sea and the local swimming spot, and not a very long walk for the children. It was her favourite place to be. All summer long she and her sisters, Joyce and Andrea, and little brother Leroy would hang out there for hours. But one hot day Andrea went up the stream a little too far.

They yelled, "Get back here Andrea, right now!" Behind her they could see a fin sticking up—it looked like a shark.

By now Joyce and Ellen were screaming, "Hurry up Andrea! It's a shark."

The water was just shallow enough to touch the bottom. Her legs were just barely touching when Leroy dog paddled to her—none of the kids could swim well. He got her close enough to shore so they could drag her out of the water. They never went back to the Landing.

Even Now You Lead Me

Come August, Ellen turned fifteen but was still unsure if she was ready for a real boyfriend as yet.

With no place to swim, Ellen decided they'd hang out in the *Granary,* as they called it. It was a cement floored garage sort of building on the old farm their parents were renting. It was a great place to listen to records on Ellen's little red record player. The sound carried well, it was like being in a dance hall practicing all their dance moves and having fun doing it. Ellen imagines she can still hear, *Crimson and Clover, Michael Jackson's Jackson Five, Rod Stewart,* and all the wonderful music that gave you an escape to a world free from all your fears, free to just dance.

Ellen's fondest memories are of all the times she and her sisters and little brother would walk everywhere they wanted to go. A simple chore like heading to *'The Old Ladies Farm'* for some fresh farm eggs was an adventure for them.

There was a store at the end of the next dirt road from theirs called, and still called, appropriately enough, *'The Store'.* Conveniently for them, there was a woods road just up the road that led to *The Store.* The children had many a joyful walk back and forth to get treats and something for Mom.

11: Ellen Meets Darcy

Ellen's father had a lot of drinking friends, including his boss at the gravel pit. Most of them had sons close to Ellen's age or a little older. She accepted a date with one of them. As Ellen says, "He was so cute and he made me feel so special when I was with him."

His name was *Darcy* and she liked him a lot. But there was this other girl that Ellen heard he was seeing when he wasn't with her. He had given that girl a ring, but Ellen's cousin Helena told her she had given it back.

One night Ellen and Darcy were driving up a dirt road and the car stalled. "We're out of gas; I guess we'll have to walk back to my parent's place."

"That sounds like fun, walking in the moonlight with you," looking softly into those gorgeous blue eyes.

It was a lovely night; the moon was shining bright as they were walking past this old one room building—an old community hall.

Darcy stopped, "Want to go in and rest a bit? I'm tired and my legs are sore"

"I guess we could if you're tired, Darcy." She felt safe with him as they walked through the papers and old books that were scattered on the floor, and they sat on a small stage at the front of the building.

"Will you lie down beside me for a little while, Ellen? I'm just too tired to walk right now," as he held his arms out for her.

He was so sweet and gentle that she melted into his open arms and they fell asleep. He was still holding her when she woke. He held her closer and whispered in her ear, "Ellen, are you ever going to let me make love to you? I love you."

Ellen whispered in his ear hoping that he would tell her that it wasn't true. "I love you too Darcy, but I'm not ready and I know you have a ring for that other girl. Are you only with me because you two broke up and I'm just your backup girl?" But he didn't answer her—he either fell asleep or pretended to.

She knew that other girl had given him what she wasn't ready to give. At that point Ellen didn't think she would *ever* be ready—her idea of what he called 'making love' was gross.

As he slept, Ellen sat up and left his side to sit down in one of the benches in the middle aisle. As she sat there she thought, 'Love—do I even know what it means? I don't know. If love means you have to do that gross stuff, I don't *ever* want to be in love.'

The morning light was coming through the doorway as she glanced through some of the old papers and books scattered over the floor. She loved looking at that kind of stuff, and still does. As she sat back down beside Darcy, he was still asleep. He was just so cute and he was a gentleman. He didn't force himself on her, yet she felt she was just a substitute for that other girl. She knew she wasn't ready yet to willingly do what he asked.

Ellen wondered, *'Is there something wrong with me, and is this all guys want?* I just don't know how I'm supposed to be.'

Darcy opened his eyes and smiled at Ellen, "Good morning beautiful."

Ellen knew, she would likely never know if Darcy had been listening that night. They walked to his dad's house just a little way up the road and his dad drove Ellen home. He did not come back for Ellen until some months later.

But Ellen will always think of Darcy as so cute and such a gentleman.

12: A Difficult Time for Ellen

For months Ellen heard nothing from Darcy, so she was enjoying hanging out with her sister, Andrea.

The next relationship Ellen had left her with many mixed emotions. She doesn't think she will ever truly understand why she let herself get involved with this guy. She has this notion that she was pushed into this relationship by her dad. She remembers not really wanting to accept a date with him, but was encouraged to go—she would have fun she was told.

She met Aaron much the same way as Darcy—his father was a drinking friend of her father. Ellen was dancing in the Granary with her sisters, Andrea and Joyce one evening to *Candida,* when Aaron and his dad drove up looking for her father.

Aaron was cute in a rugged sort of way—shaggy brown hair, blue eyes, and a whiskery baby face. His brown corduroy jeans and blazer looked good on him with a white t-shirt and a gold chain on his neck.

Ellen ignored them as they passed by the Granary to the front door of the house and knocked on the porch door. Aaron's father looked really scary—like the Hunch Back of Notre-Dame. They knew the visitors were in the house drinking and listening to her Dad playing his fiddle. Ellen didn't like the fiddle back then—she assumes because she associated it with men drinking and acting gross. She wanted to be as far away as possible from them. The girls stayed in the Granary until they left.

Her father must have told Aaron that she hung around with her cousin Deanna and Deanna's boyfriend Gary. The very next Sunday a car drove up the lane right to the front door, and Deanna came up. She yells, "Ellen, want to come for a drive with Gary and me? We have someone who wants to meet you."

Ellen was going to say *no,* but since Deanna was present, she went. That evening was fun, they just drove around and listened to the radio and chatted.

Gary stopped at a corner store and Aaron asked if Ellen would like something.

"Pepsi and plain chips would be nice, thank you," she said as she noticed he had the two first fingers missing at the first joint on his right hand.

Well Ellen thought, 'He might be a nice guy but still I don't want to be alone with him.'

As long as Deanna and Gary came along, Ellen was comfortable with Aaron. That way she didn't feel like she would be pressured into something she didn't want to do. They dated for a couple of weekends, but when he came by himself to pick her up, she was reluctant.

Ellen's Mom had some fried chicken she thought would be a nice treat for Aaron. She ushered Ellen out the door with it saying, "Run along dear, Aaron is waiting, now don't be late and have fun. Love you."

"Thanks Mom, love you too, I won't be late." Ellen said as Aaron leaned over, opening the door for her from his driver's seat.

"Hi, Aaron, Mom sent this for you, its fried chicken." She blurted nervously, then trying to relax, "Are we picking up Deanna and Gary?"

"No, not tonight Ellen, they had other plans, so I thought we could go for a drive." He said in that tone she recognized of someone that had been drinking.

"Ok Aaron, that sounds like fun. It's a beautiful night isn't it?" trying not to sound nervous.

As Ellen settled in her seat she offered Aaron a piece of her Mom's chicken, "Want to try a piece, it's really good, Mom thought you would like some?"

His reply wasn't what she expected or wanted, "Just put it in the dash Ellen, maybe I'll eat it later, or you can eat it."

As she opened the dash she felt both sad and insulted that he didn't take the chicken and say how great her Mom's cooking was.

All she could think to say was "Where are we going Aaron? Mom told me not to be late."

He started sounding annoyed, "Ellen, we're just going for a drive, all right? I'll get you home early."

Ellen and her family had moved to the old farmhouse about two years before this. She was still unsure of the dirt roads surrounding their community. She stayed silent for a few minutes and waited for him to say where they were going. Instead of saying anything he reaches under the car seat, and pulls out a bottle of hard liquor, like the kind her Dad drank, and glared at her as he offered her a drink.

Ellen pushed the bottle away and said, "I don't drink, Aaron and I don't like driving with anyone when they drink—it scares me. Perhaps you'd better just take me home." As soon as she said it she knew this wasn't what he wanted to hear.

He pushed the accelerator to the floor and roared at her, "You little tramp, don't play all innocent with me. I know you're not, so I am going to *get some* or I'll just drive until the road ends, it's your choice. So what is it, *yes* or *no*?" as he pushed harder on the pedal.

The car was swerving on the gravel road. By this time Ellen was screaming "No, slow down! You're going to kill us Aaron; I just want to go home."

As all the fears came back—she was afraid he would kill them if she didn't submit. Like a child, she huddled in the seat and said, "Alright, just slow down and you can have me." Ellen could not look at him; she was dead to all emotions except fear.

"That's more like it; don't worry you're going to love it." Aaron said as he slowed down and turned the car in the middle of the road, and pulled to the side.

The moon was shining and she hoped maybe another car would come and he wouldn't do that to her. No car came as she sat there frozen.

Aaron got out of the car and came around to her side and grabbed her hand and pulled her out of the car and said, "Get in the back, there's more room."

He had stopped the car at the cemetery a few miles from Ellen's home, but which way was home? She wasn't sure.

She tried mentally to block him out as he got on top of her, his breath reeking of hard liquor, as he mumbled something in her ear.

When it was over he said proudly, "I knew you were easy, you're nothing but a whore."

Ellen stayed silent as he fell asleep on top of her in a drunken stupor; she had to get out of that car before he woke up. She wriggled out from under him, leaving him passed out in the back seat.

Ellen straightened her clothes as best she could and looked for the only guidance she could depend on and prayed,

"Dear God,

Please forgive me for letting this happen. Show me how to get home. Walk with me. Don't leave me God. I'm sorry. Help me Lord. I'm afraid of the dark. Please stay with me."

Amen

As she looked around, the moon smiled, making it easy to see. She tried to think which way home was from there. She remembered she and her friends had walked to the store on the main road, and the main road was toward the shore. Ellen was afraid to walk past that cemetery anyway. She looked the other way and thought to herself, 'Maybe the dirt road Aaron turned on back there will get me to The Store; I can find my way home from there.'

Well, Ellen wasn't alone! The *Lord* walked with her down that otherwise creepy road, as she cried, made promises to Him, and begged forgiveness—forgiveness for what she wasn't sure. But it surely felt like she had done wrong and she just wanted to make it right.

Ellen could hear birds chirping in the woods, 'That's fine, just keep walking,' she thought as the glow of a street light on the corner assured her she was going in the right direction—well at least the easiest way she knew of to get home.

She walked past the Old Store and headed for the next dirt road that would take her home.

Thoughts flooded her head, 'How am I going to explain this to Mom. She told me to be home early. I promised Mom. I can't tell Mom what happened, I'm so ashamed *Lord.* Lead me, help me, and don't leave me.'

She must have walked for hours but she did make it home. (Ellen realizes now that her route home was the longest way, the cemetery road was only about two or three miles from home). Although the walk gave her lots of time to think, she was more confused than ever about men. The only thing in her life she was sure of was her trust in God to stay with her, no matter what men did to her. She was exhausted but she ran up her driveway and checked the front door to see if it was locked. Her Mom had left it open for her. She crept inside and knelt down on her knees and prayed,

"Dear Jesus,

Thank you for taking me home and if You'll not let this foolish mistake leave me pregnant, you can have my first-born."

Amen

At that time Ellen didn't have any idea what that statement meant. Remembering this she says now, "I mean, I know *Jesus* must have understood me better then I understood myself."

Ellen had been quite used to crying quietly with her secrets but this one was really big. She tried washing the filthy feeling away, but it wouldn't go away. She finally crawled into bed and sobbed quietly to sleep.

13: Ellen Reluctantly Forgives

You'd think the relationship with Aaron would have ended there, but not so! The next day brought no questions about why Ellen had been late, so she said nothing. She did not expect Aaron to show his face again—wow, was she wrong!

Not only did he come back, he arrived all clean and shaven, talking to Ellen's father in the yard.

'Maybe Dad will make him go away,' she thought, forgetting that she hadn't told anyone what had happened to her.

Her father came in the house saying, "Ellen, Aaron would like to talk to you."

"I don't want to talk to him Dad, I don't think I like him," not knowing what else to say, hoping he would just leave.

"Ellen, give the boy a chance. He likes you. Get out there and talk to him," pushing her out the door, while Mom washed the dishes saying nothing.

Aaron smiled at her with an *I won* look as he pleaded, "Ellen please get in, I just want to talk to you."

"I don't want to talk to you—you called me a whore, and easy and other bad stuff," she said trembling, trying to be strong.

"Ellen, I'm so sorry I called you anything, I promise I'll never do that again. I really like you. Will you forgive me and let me make it up to you?" he said in a tender voice that was making her believe his words.

"Come on, get in and we'll go pick up Deanna and Gary, all right Ellen?" as he leaned across and opened the door for her. Ellen's Dad and Mom were looking out the kitchen window at them, waving for her to run along.

Ellen reflects back thinking, *'At fifteen I guess you do tend to believe someone if they tell you they love you or like you and give them a second chance.'*

Aaron did pick up Deanna and Gary that evening. Ellen wanted to confide in Deanna but she couldn't bring herself to talk about it. She was too ashamed of what had happened to her. They went for a drive, and had fun that night and the next couple of weekends.

One weekend though, Aaron showed up alone and asked Ellen to go for a drive to meet his parents. She should have said *no* but she didn't, remembering his Dad looked like the Hunch Back. Aaron's house was as scary looking as his Dad—something like the Amityville house.

His brother, Freeman, who always walked everywhere actually had a hunched back too, and never said a word, making him just as scary. Just knowing this, Ellen thought she must have been crazy to consider letting Aaron take her near the place.

Aaron had just told her his Mom had left his Dad so he lived there with just his two brothers and his father.

As Ellen looked out the car window at the dreary old house a chill ran up her spine and she was reluctant when Aaron opened her door reaching for her hand, "Let's go in for a few minutes Ellen."

"I don't think anyone is home, Aaron. I'll meet them another time." Hoping he would agree with her and take her home.

"Oh come on. They won't bite you, let's go," as he grabbed her hand and hauled her out of the car.

"Alright, just for a few minutes," praying this wasn't another mistake.

"Anyone home, I want you to meet Ellen." Aaron yelled but no one answered.

"Well we should just go; maybe Deanna and Gary will want to go for a drive," really not wanting to be inside that house that was as dreary inside as out.

She could tell only guys lived there—everything was a mess, dishes everywhere, nothing looked clean.

"First let me show you my room." Aaron said taking her hand and leading her into a small bedroom right of the kitchen.

The room was dark so Aaron lit a candle and set it on a dresser in the corner.

"Now isn't this nice Ellen? It's like we're married. Come sit on the bed with me." Again taking her hand and easing her to his side.

He kissed Ellen and, *before she could say anything, he was undressing her and whispering in her ear that he loved her.* He held her close under the heavy quilt whispering, "I wish we could stay like this forever Ellen, don't you?"

"Sure Aaron, but shouldn't we be going? Your Dad might be here soon, I told Mom I wouldn't be late." She whispered hoping no one would walk in and find them.

Ellen barely had the words out of her mouth and a car drove in. Aaron said quickly, "Get dressed Ellen—it's my brother."

They were all in the kitchen before Ellen and Aaron came out of his room. His brothers looked at Ellen like she was a piece of meat ready to be eaten. His Dad eyed her up and down and said, "Who is this little darling, Aaron?" and offered Ellen his hand.

Aaron introduced Ellen to them saying, "This is Ellen, Dad." "Ellen, this is my brother Sam and my little brother Freeman."

Sam and his Father were obviously drinking, for when Ellen shook Sam's hand he held on to hers and pulled her towards him and kissed her and then pushed her towards Freeman, who was more of a gentleman than any of them—he said and did nothing to Ellen.

Aaron finally stepped in and said, "That's enough guys, Ellen is all mine." "Say good-night. I have to take her home."

Ellen was so relieved to get out of that house, she promised herself she'd never go there again.

That one line—*I wish we could stay like this forever Ellen, don't you?*—stayed in the back of Ellen's mind to this day. Maybe he meant it. *Maybe there was something wrong with her. Why didn't she feel the way he said he did? All she knew was she felt no emotions.* By then she had learned to block out anything that brought her back to any of those bad things, almost as if she was not there. She knew these things happened to her, even as scared as she was when Aaron did that to her in his car the first time. She put it aside and went back with him—why?

Take for instance the 1987 movie *Dirty Dancing*. Ellen still can't take her eyes off the hero. 'Oh my God, if someone like him actually existed—someone who would actually take me in his arms, dance with me, make me feel beautiful, I would never let him go. Maybe I'll always be happier in a fantasy world, I'm not sure.' Obviously a bit of that young girl still lives in Ellen.

From that night, Ellen decided she would never go on another date unless they had someone else along. When Aaron came to pick her up the next weekend, she told him Andrea was coming with them if it was alright with him.

His response surprised her, "Sure, why not, I thought we would go to the Drive-in. I think Deanna and Gary want to come too."

"Thank you Aaron, climb in Andrea." Ellen said still finding it hard to believe he said *yes*.

They had fun that night, and Andrea was so excited to be out to a movie with her big sister.

Everyone thought she was the cutest girl. Ellen actually enjoyed herself and felt at ease all that evening.

The following Saturday Aaron arrived early and informed Ellen that they were going to the beach with Deanna and Gary.

Ellen said, "That sounds like fun Aaron, and Andrea loves the beach, I'll go get her."

When Ellen and Andrea came back to the car, Aaron had an annoyed look, "Don't you have little friends to hang out with, Andrea?"

Andrea giggled as she climbed in the back seat and said, "Ellen is my best friend, Aaron."

That whole evening Aaron tolerated Andrea, but Ellen could tell he wasn't too enthusiastic about her accompanying them anymore. She knew it was just a matter of time before he would tell her Andrea wouldn't be allowed to come.

Well, Ellen was right. While Deanna was inside getting a sweater, Andrea was chatting away about her day to Aaron when he freaked out and lost it, "Will you shut up Andrea! I don't want to hear whatever it is you're yapping about—I'm taking you home."

Before he could say another word to Andrea, Ellen stopped him, yelling in his face, "If you're taking Andrea home, you're tak-

Even Now You Lead Me

ing me home too, and don't bother picking me up again—we're through! Andrea is my little sister, and you're scaring her. I'll take her anywhere, anytime with me."

Deanna came out swinging her sweater, "What's wrong Ellen? Why is Andrea crying? Is she alright?"

"Oh Aaron, decided he doesn't like Andrea's company and he's taking her home, so he can take me home too. You guys can still go with him if you want though." trying not to upset Deanna.

"We can go another time Ellen; it's no fun without you at the beach or anywhere else. I have stuff to do anyway. You take care of Andrea and we'll see you guys soon." as she gave Ellen a hug.

"Thanks Deanna. You're the best. See you later." As she got back in Aaron's car and waved.

Well Ellen had stood up for herself and Andrea, and he took them home alright, but apparently he didn't think she was serious about ending the relationship because he said, "I'll see you next weekend Ellen."

"Don't bother Aaron, I don't want to see you anymore. My little sister is in there crying. She doesn't know why you're mad at her. It doesn't matter what you think of her, we won't be seeing you again. Good night," as she slammed the car door and ran to the house.

Aaron left and it was a long while before he would return.

Deanna felt so bad about their bad weekend that she called, "Listen Ellen, I know you're upset and I feel responsible for hooking you and Aaron up. Some guys can be such jerks, so let me make it up to you."

"That's alright Deanna; it's not your fault. I should have said *no* from the start," not wanting her best friend feeling that any of her own mistakes were her friend's fault.

"I'm not taking *no* for an answer. You're coming with us this weekend; you're not going to stay home because of that jerk," Deanna insisted.

"Oh, alright 'Mother', I'll go with you guys." she said, laughing at her mother-hen friend.

"That's better, we'll have fun, and you never know what might turn up." She giggled in that way she had when she wanted to cheer Ellen up.

14: Helena and Ellen go Dancing

The next weekend Ellen was all prettied up to enjoy the evening with Deanna and Gary when the phone rang. It was her first cousin *Helena* begging Ellen to join her and sleep over at her house.

'I swear if it wasn't for my two best friends, (Helena and Deanna) I'd have no life at all,' Ellen thought, all smiles.

Ellen has cousins that are double-first-cousins—their parents are three brothers who married three sisters. Ellen thinks that makes them pretty special. Out of all her double-first-cousins, Deanna and Ellen look the most alike.

"Helena, I kind of promised Deanna I'd go with them tonight, she feels she has to cheer me up after last weekend."

"Ellen, call her and tell her you and I are going to the *Roll-A-Way* tonight. Dad said he'd drive us in. The band is so great, and they play that horn you're so dreamy after. Come on, we can show off those moves we practiced on the dance floor, remember? Please, please Ellen, it won't be any fun without you, pretty please," she pleaded, not making it easy for Ellen to say *no*; after all she really loved that dreamy golden horn.

"Alright Helena, I'll call Deanna and tell her we'll go another night, ok? I'll call you right back," Ellen said knowing Helena knew she couldn't resist that golden sound that seemed to sweep Ellen of her feet to her own fantasy world.

Deanna as usual, just wanted Ellen to be happy, "You guys go, and show them how it's done. Just give me a call if you need me, Ellen; love you girl; see you soon.

"Thanks Deanna; love you back girl; I'll call you." Ellen felt so lucky to have her cousins always there for her.

Ellen called Helena back and she and her Dad picked Ellen up. Then they were off to Helena's place to try on different outfits, do their hair, and try their dance moves in front of the mirror. Satisfied they looked great, the girls were ready—maybe—for the most exciting night of their lives—well, Ellen's anyway. She had never been to the *Roll-A-Way,* and her heart was pounding as they arrived at the entrance.

Helena told her dad that they would get a drive home. He said, "You two be careful and if you need me you have change for the phone. Don't stay out too late girls, alright?"

"Ok Dad, we'll be good, love you," Helena said as she hurriedly shut the car door, grabbed Ellen's hand, and headed for the entrance, "Hurry Ellen; we don't want to miss a thing, do we?"

"I guess not!" Ellen said, laughing at her crazy cousin.

As they entered the room the band was getting ready to play. Helena had been there before so she knew what to expect. Ellen on the other hand was about to be left breathless. The girls were all mingling to the right and the guys to the left. The lights on the ceiling came on, revolving red, blue, yellow, green; she was amazed by it all.

Then, "Ellen, watch this guy as we walk by him—just follow me." Helena giggled.

Ellen had no idea what to expect. This guy was sitting on the side of the hallway leading up to the dance floor leaving just enough room to squeeze by. She couldn't help but notice how absolutely gorgeous he was, and he obviously was aware of that. Feet dangling over the ledge, confidence oozed out of him.

Time stopped as Ellen tried to capture his image—from head to toe he was perfect in her eyes; shoulder length light brown tussled hair that covered one eye until he looked up and flipped it back revealing two icy blue eyes. His orange muscle shirt showed off his golden tanned chest and arms, tucked into perfect fitting blue jeans. His pant legs pulled down over his shiny black boots made his whole look like someone out of the movie *Dirty Dancing*.

"Ellen, wake up. Come on, and watch this." Helena said as she grabbed Ellen's hand heading towards him.

"I'm coming Helena." She shook herself back to reality.

Helena let go of Ellen's hand as she was about to pass by him. Ellen's felt her mouth must have been hanging open as she watched him reach for Helena's hand and pull her towards him. He then kissed Helena and whispered something in her ear and

Even Now You Lead Me

she looked at Ellen motioning her over as she headed off to the dance floor.

Chills ran up Ellen's spine as she moved closer to him thinking that he might introduce himself, maybe shake her hand and that would be it.

Instead, he reaches for her hand, lightly kisses it, wraps his arm around her waist and gently draws Ellen close to him whispering in her ear, "Hello beautiful; Ellen isn't it? I'm Martin; this is your first time here, isn't it?" he said while still holding her close.

Ellen nodded *yes*, still mesmerized by this dream guy that was, oh, so real. Then Martin, still with his arm around her waist, gently places his other hand on the back of Ellen's head. He draws her closer to him as she melted in his arms, closed her eyes as their lips met in the most passionate, gentle kiss that she could ever have imagined.

She did not want it to end as he slowly released her. As their eyes met she wondered does he treat all the girls like this or was she really special to him.

Martin then takes her hand asking, "Could I see you maybe next week-end Ellen?"

She looked into those gorgeous blue eyes saying, "I'd love to Martin."

"Where do you live Ellen?" he asks still holding her hand.

"218 Mill Road—not far from the post office." Ellen said, thinking that sounded a bit desperate.

"How about I pick you up at eight next Saturday?" as he kissed Ellen's hand. "Sound good to you Ellen?"

"*Yes*, sounds great Martin, see you Saturday," she gushed as Martin let go of her hand and she headed off to join Cousin Helena on the dance floor.

"Helena, Martin just asked me out Saturday. Is that alright with you?" Ellen said hesitantly.

"It's fine by me, but I wouldn't hold my breath waiting for Martin to pick you up, Ellen." Helena said a bit sarcastically.

"Why wouldn't he? He said I was beautiful. Are you maybe just a little jealous he didn't ask you?" Ellen pouted like a spoiled child.

"Ellen, you're fifteen, I'm seventeen, and I've already been stood up by Martin! He gave me the same line as he gave you. I thought he was wonderful too. I'm just telling you he won't show up. That's how he gets his kicks. I know he's gorgeous, I'm sorry Ellen. I should have warned you first, and then maybe you'd see what he's really like." She gave Ellen a hug.

"You're wrong. Martin likes me and he will come," Ellen said trying to sound confident.

"Well I hope so. Just remember what I said, and don't be too disappointed if he doesn't. If he's such a great guy, why isn't he up here with you dancing? He's likely still out there greeting more girls. Oh Ellen, don't get hung up on Martin. He's really not worth it." Helena sounded like a big sister to Ellen.

"Let's just dance." Ellen pleaded not wanting to talk about it anymore, and hoping she was wrong about Martin. (Incidentally, she never did see Martin on the dance floor that evening after he asked her out for the next weekend.)

As they took up their positions the band (*THE BLUE CRYSTALS*) played a slow dance. So they just mingled, then Helena struck up a conversation with some guy she knew. Ellen wandered back to the floor and danced with some girls that liked how she danced.

Ellen was having fun dancing when Helena taps her on the shoulder and whispers, "Nick wants to drive me home later and I said *yes*, I really like him. Do you mind if I go?"

"Ok Helena, but how am I going to get home, and I thought you wanted me to sleep over," not sure of what to do next.

"My friend Allan said he would be happy to take you home. We can have a sleepover next weekend, alright?"

"Where is this Allan, Helena? Can I trust him?" Ellen said very hesitantly.

Just then that dreamy horn was whisking her away to a fantasy world and everything seemed fine as Helena says, "I'll go get him, Ellen, I'll be right back.

"If you say so, I guess it will be fine." she said as she swayed back and forth to that heavenly sound.

Within seconds she was back with a tall, dark haired guy with glasses who looked kind of geeky to Ellen.

"Ellen this is Allan; Allan this is Ellen my best friend. She says she would appreciate it, if you would give her a drive home."

"Hello Ellen, nice to meet you, I would be honored to drive such a beautiful girl as you home, if you would allow me" Confident yet nervous at the same time.

"Nice to meet you Allan, thank you, but I don't want you to go out of your way. I live out in the country." Ellen said still unsure if she should be accepting a ride from someone she barely knew.

"That's not a problem Ellen. You'll have to show me how to get there though; I'm not familiar with driving down there," he said very politely.

"Ok Allan, would you like to dance?" Ellen asked unsure if she really wanted to dance with a guy a foot taller than herself.

"Thank you Ellen, but dancing is not one of my accomplishments. I'll just hang around and watch you guys and when you're ready to go home I'll be over there." He said mildly, more or less letting her off the hook.

"Ok Allan, if you're sure. You're very kind. Thank you," she said hoping she wasn't being rude; he did seem like a nice guy.

"I'll be fine, you have fun Ellen, and I'll be around." Allan sounded more like a brother watching over her.

"See you after then, Allan." Ellen danced her way back to the girls.

Helena danced with Nick the rest of the evening, and, as for Ellen she doesn't remember having danced with a single guy that night or any other night. She guesses she was never meant to have that fantasy come true.

Helena eventually came over to Ellen and said, "We're leaving soon. You still alright with Allan taking you home?"

As Ellen looked around the room she said to Helena, "Do you see Allan? He told me he would be around when I was ready to go home."

Helena looks around and says, "I think he's out in the parking lot talking to some of the guys while he's waiting. Let's go out and see. Nick's out there too."

Well things took an abrupt turn when they reached the parking lot.

Helena grabs Ellen's hand and says, "Come on Ellen, I'll take you out to find him."

She led her down the stairs and around the back of the Roll-A-Way to the parking lot where the guys were supposed to be. There was a black van parked of to the side of the building under the street light. There must have been ten or more teenagers jammed in that van. One of them was Martin and he spotted Ellen and asked to speak to her. She hesitated for a minute as Helena whispered to just ignore him.

Ellen thought about it and said, "Helena, if I don't talk to him, I'll never know if he was serious about asking me out. I'll be right back. Find Allan and come get me."

"Alright Ellen, don't you let him talk you into anything stupid. I'll see if Allan is over there and be right back," as she ran over to a car parked across from the van.

As Ellen got closer to the van, Martin reaches for her saying, "Climb in Ellen, we're going down town for drinks and a burger—you'll have fun."

"I'm sure that would be fun, but I don't drink, and my drive will be here in a minute. I just wanted to say goodnight, Martin," Ellen said waiting for him to reassure her that they had a date the following Saturday.

Well, he did reassure Ellen as he said, "You're sure you won't come with us. I'll still see you Saturday, ok Ellen?"

Relieved that he remembered, she blushed and answered quickly, "Sure Martin, I'll be waiting."

Martin reached out for her hand and kissed it gently saying, "See you Saturday, beautiful."

As they drove away Helena came running back out of breath, "You see that car over there, Ellen. Don't you recognize it?"

At that moment it began to rain and glancing at the car she couldn't believe it—it was Aaron, and her thoughts immediately were, 'This can't be good.'

Out of breath Helena says, "It is Aaron, and he's looking for you."

"Well I certainly don't want to see him. Did you find Allan yet? All I want right now is to go home," she said frantically.

"Allan is over there in that brown van across the street. I told him to wait for you. Nick is sitting in with him while he waits," reassuring Ellen that they wouldn't leave her alone with Aaron.

Ellen turned to see if Aaron was going to leave, but he rolls down the window and yells at them, "I need to talk to you two now."

Helena turns to Ellen and says, "Come on. I'll help you get rid of him, Ellen."

It was raining pretty hard and they were getting soaked. Ellen wanted Aaron to just leave her alone, so they walked over to the car window, and Helena spoke up and said, "What do you want Aaron? Ellen and I already have a ride home; she doesn't want anything to do with you? So why are you here?"

"I want Ellen to tell me she doesn't want to see me to my face. Tell me, Ellen, or are you too busy making it with those guys to bother with a real man." He roared at her, obviously drunk and jealous.

"Aaron, that remark doesn't deserve an answer, and it is none of your business what I do now or ever. I don't like your attitude nor do I appreciate you following me here and accusing me of anything; we're through! I thought I made that clear already." Ellen said as sternly as she could.

"I'm sorry, Ellen, get in, your soaked, we'll talk about this and I'll drive you home, please," Aaron pleaded trying desperately to get her to go with him.

"No, Aaron, I have a drive home with Helena's friend and he's waiting for me. I told you before, I don't like driving with someone who's drinking. It scares me. Just go home, Aaron, and leave me alone."

"Never mind talking to him, Ellen. He doesn't get it. Go home, Aaron, and sober up and stop bothering Ellen. She told you she was through with you, now go," Helena roared at Aaron like a protective big sister, to Ellen's relief.

"I'll go, but I'll see you next weekend, Ellen." Aaron said as he squealed his tires and tore out of the parking lot and down the street.

Helena and Ellen let out an exhausted *arrgh* as they watched him go.

"Do you think he will come back or try to follow me or something Helena?" not knowing what to expect next.

"No, I don't think you'll have to worry about him tonight. Come on, I'll walk you over to Allan's van and get you home." She grabbed Ellen's hand, heading to Allan's parked van.

They were pretty soggy looking characters, but the rain had eased off by then. As Helena opened the door for Ellen, Allan reached out his hand helping her into the van saying, "Is everything alright girls? Nick and I didn't want to interfere, but we watched and were ready if he got out of that car."

"Yeah, we're fine, Allan. Ellen's just a bit upset with that jerk that just left." Helena said speaking for her again, but she didn't mind—she didn't feel like explaining.

"Well Ellen, you'll be fine with Allan, he'll get you home safely. I'm going to go with Nick now, alright Ellen? I'll see you tomorrow Ellen, night, night, love you girl." Helena said blowing a kiss as she went to join Nick who had brought his car just in front of Allan's van.

"Thanks Helena, love you too, see you tomorrow." She blew a kiss back.

"You sure you don't mind taking me home, Allan? It's way out in the country," Ellen asked hoping he wasn't expecting more than a thank-you from her.

"No problem Ellen. Just show me the way and I'll be glad to drive you home." He offered Ellen his jacket. "You're soaked Ellen. Here put this on until we get you home."

"Thank you Allan, that's very sweet of you. Well I'm not great with directions, but I know we just follow the main highway out of town and keep going until we get to my dirt road," Ellen said, feeling kind of dumb.

All the way out from town they barely spoke, other than Allan asking if they were still going in the right direction and Ellen telling him to just keep going until they were nearing her little community. "See that church on the left Allan? Mill Road is the next left and the house is a little way on the left. I'll tell you when we get there, OK?"

"Ok Ellen, turn left here right?" He said so politely.

"*Yes* Allan, thanks again for taking me home." Ellen said thinking, 'Is he for real?'

"There, next left is my lane; I can walk up from here, Allan, thanks again." Ellen said.

As she leaned over to kiss his cheek, he wrapped his arms around her and kissed her saying, "You're so beautiful Ellen, can I see you again? I'll gladly pick you up—just say the word."

"I can't, Allan, I have a date next weekend and it wouldn't be right to break it," trying not to insult him yet not encourage him.

Ellen was wearing a little purple, orange, and green diagonally striped stretch mini dress and it was beginning to slip up as he was trying to hold on to her so she said, "Allan I have to go. If Dad sees us he'll be down the lane before you have time to back up and he'll be mad," as she slid out of his arms, onto the floor and out the door, running up the lane, not looking back.

Once she got in the house the lights were out and everyone was asleep. She looked out the window to see Allan backing out and leaving. She breathed a sigh of relief and headed off to bed.

15: No Dream Date for Ellen

Well, Saturday arrived; Ellen spent all day deciding what to wear and just the right shoes to go with it. Her long red hair was shining, as she thought to herself, 'I look pretty cool. Martin and I are going to have a great time.'

Poor little Ellen sat there all evening watching out her bedroom window. Waiting for her prince to come sweep her of her feet. She cried, as she thought perhaps he didn't get her address right, or maybe he was just late. Finally, at ten o'clock she had to face the fact that she had been stood up. How was she going to face Helena?

Well Helena was over at Ellen's house the next day when she told her.

"I told you he wouldn't show up Ellen, it's all a game to Martin. That's how he gets his kicks."

"Maybe he'll come next Saturday. He was so nice to me," hoping Helena would agree with her.

"Just forget him Ellen. He's not worth wasting your weekend waiting for him to show up. He's not coming," she said in her 'I told you so' tone.

"I guess you're right. What do you want to do next weekend?" trying to sound like it didn't matter anymore.

"Well, why don't we go swimming at the pool—that cute guy Farren might be there? I think he likes you. What do you say? Want to go with me girl?" Helena was coaching Ellen like she was a little girl.

Ellen couldn't help but laugh, "Sure, why not, you old hen."

They ended up having a pillow fight. Her Mom wasn't very pleased when the feathers drifted out of Ellen's door and down the stairs.

Mothers know how it is, though. They were teenage girls once too, weren't they?

As for Martin, you guessed it, that night was their only night. Ellen doesn't really have any regrets. Martin gave her a dream kiss and she will always have that tucked away deep in her memory. Does every girl save a memory like this, tucked away for safe keeping? *Just for her* to remind her, that for that one night she believed she was beautiful to that handsome stranger!

Martin was a handsome stranger, but that's all he ever would be. He disappointed Ellen by not showing up, yet in the back of her mind she was secretly relieved. She has the memory of a perfect kiss with none of the realities that a real relationship would bring.

Fifteen is such a hard age, you don't really know how to cope with all these adult situations you're faced with, then you have to cope with the way you handled each situation.

Ellen says from experience with dealing with young people over the years, "Being a woman, I can't honestly see the guy's side of these situations. I do have two sons and know most of their friends and they have come to me for advice when they have relationship problems. I can understand their positions because I know them and they, too, often need a shoulder and a friend to listen to them.

A fifteen, sixteen or even seventeen-year-old girl meets a gorgeous guy and gets her heart broken. When he tells her he loves her, she usually believes him. She commits to a relationship with him and it lasts but a short time. Maybe he finds another girl, gets bored with her, feels tied down with her or whatever. Regardless, she is young and gives her heart willingly to the smooth talking, handsome stranger, only to have it broken.

At fifteen you don't feel comfortable confiding in your parents or grandparents and Ellen understands that. She went through that too, but she honestly feels if she had to do it over again she would welcome the comfort of her Mom's advice and the love and peace she could have had from confiding in her! She missed all that love due to the abuse that left her alone with those dark secrets that in her mind she had to keep a secret.

There are many girls that grew up this way, who would prefer a fantasy world rather than their own. Ellen's dreams are still of her dream world of perfection and no tears. That's a description of Heaven isn't it? Moms would love to see their little girls not suffer in any way as they did, but they do have to let you grow.

Wouldn't it be a better way if we could communicate honestly with each other? When you have a problem that's just too big, don't be afraid to tell the one you trust—don't go it alone.

Ellen concludes, "Now that's off my chest I hope you can understand how keeping things bottled up inside you can keep you from ever finding a lasting real relationship. Keeping these things in the back of our minds keeps us from enjoying our lives, and it will forever influence how we live if we let it rule us."

16: Quiet Times and Just Being Happy

After her ended relationship with Aaron, and her disappointment with Martin, Ellen just enjoyed hanging out with Andrea, and tending to her new baby sister.

Winter was upon them, but they all kept busy dancing, reading, drawing, and listening to their favorite radio station. They'd often stay up late telling ghost stories, and with bedtime snacks that Mom would bring them.

She will never forget the hot bowls of Campbell's vegetable soup mixed with canned milk and homemade biscuits. Then for a change Mom would bring them Heinz tomato soup with canned milk and homemade bread and butter all mixed together. It remains a favourite lunch any time of day for Ellen.

She can still hear her Mom yelling from downstairs, "Now eat girls. No jumping on the bed, and don't stay up all night. Good night, love yahs."

There is just no way to jump on your bed quietly, is there? Nevertheless, they always ate every drop of their lunch and set their bowls on the dresser. Then they jumped and flipped on that old bed until they were exhausted. Next they talked about boys, music, and their latest dance moves. They would lie on the bed, one going each way, usually falling asleep scratching each other's feet.

One of Ellen's favorite pastimes was sewing. Her mom showed her how to make birch bark canoes to hang on the wall. You get a large piece of birch bark and draw an outline of a canoe with both halves of the canoe not cut out at the bottom. Then you fold the two halves together and sew both ends up to the end of the curl at each end of the canoe. From each end of the canoe a woven thread is strung to hang the canoe on the wall. On each canoe when it was finished you'd take different coloured ink pens and write things like *Deanna loves?* or *Helena loves?* or whatever. Some of the girls have kept their canoes till this day.

Ellen loved making her own clothes out of anything she could find upstairs in the spare room where Mom stored old clothes and stuff. Miniskirts and bellbottoms were the rage, and Ellen's creations were quite popular. Tight-legged pants were transformed into bellbottoms. She cut them of at the knee and sewed on a flared bell cut out of old dresses, skirts, etc. The bolder the color the better. Also the bigger the bell the better, making for a very *'in'* pair of Bell Bottom Pants.

Ellen's miniskirts were usually cut from old long skirts she found in the attic. Her favorite skirt was a lime green one she found up there—alterations were simply to take it in to make it tight and take it up to make it short. Her cousins thought Ellen's skirts were awesome, so she went to work and whipped up more of her fabulous creations. A girl can't have too many fancy things in her wardrobe.

They were not that well off, but the clothes she made meant a lot to her. Especially since her cousins and family liked them—that was all that really mattered.

Winter was slowly passing, and boyfriends were still on the back burner for Ellen. She really didn't mind—she was content just hanging around with her cousins and Andrea.

With the arrival of spring her Dad's friends were coming out of the woodwork. So she began hiding out at her cousin's house again. Andrea usually stayed home with Mom.

Ellen says, "I feel selfish now, seeing that I used to take her with me for protection when I had a boyfriend, then, when I had none, she got left home."

17: Ellen's Meet's Farren

One evening Ellen went for a drive with Helena and her boyfriend Thomas. They stopped at his house for something, and it just so happened they introduced Ellen to his brother Farren. He was the one Helena said she thought liked Ellen.

Ellen offered him her hand as he said, "Helena has told me all about you and I was wondering if you'd like to come out with me this evening? We're just going for a drive and stuff."

"She did, did she?" as she looks over her glasses at Helena, who was giggling.

"Ellen, it was all good, really. You know me, girl." Helena teased.

Ellen didn't see any reason why she shouldn't go. He seemed very nice and cute too, so she agreed saying, "That sounds like fun. Farren. I'd love to go."

They all had fun that night, driving around talking, and getting to know each other. Helena and Thomas treated Ellen and Farren to a burger at the Drive-in restaurant in town. Then they headed back for home.

They drove Ellen home first "Thanks so much you guys, I had a wonderful time. Goodnight you two. Goodnight Farren, I had an awesome time."

Farren had a car of his own that he told her he had to do some work to. "Ellen, when I get my car going will you come out with me again?"

Ellen liked him so much she said, without hesitation. "Sure, Farren, that would be fun. You call me when you get it fixed."

About two weeks later Farren called saying, "Hi Ellen. It's Farren. I got my car fixed. Would you like to come out with me this evening? Are you busy?"

Ellen replied, "I'm glad you have your car fixed, and *no*, I'm not doing anything tonight. I'd love to go out with you."

"Wow, that's great, I'll pick you up at eight, ok?"

"That's fine, I'll be ready, bye."

"See you soon Ellen, bye."

18: Ellen's Date

You know how your heart races and a lump seems to be in your throat when you are about to start a new relationship? That's how Ellen was that evening, happy yet nervous as she sat at her bedroom window waiting for him to arrive.

When Farren's old car rattled up the driveway, she had goose bumps everywhere as she watched him get out of his car.

Farren had kind of a country-boy look that she found comforting. He was very slim with a fair complexion, black wavy hair combed to the side in Elvis style—blue eyes and a heart-warming smile that curled up to the right side of his mouth. His blue denim jacket and red chequered shirt sleeves pushed up to his elbows and denim jeans looked awesome on him.

Ellen quickly checked her hair and made sure her outfit looked just right in her full length mirror. Her favourite lime green mini-skirt, gold chain belt, and matching green–and–brown striped turtle neck with a tiny gold chain at the neck attached with small gold buttons and green sandals). '*Yes*, just fine.'

She dashed down the stairs and out to the kitchen. Mom was in the kitchen washing the supper dishes, so Ellen opened the door for Farren.

He offered her his hand, "Ellen, you look so pretty. Would you like to go for a drive to town, maybe grab a burger?"

"Sure Farren, I'd love to," as he walked her to his car and opened the door for her.

Farren and Ellen went to town and had their burgers and fries. He ordered a sloppy old *Big Mac* for himself and for Ellen, her favourite, a *Quarter Pounder*, no cheese, no pickles, raw onions, ketchup, mayo, and mustard. She still loves those *Quarter Pounders* as much as she dislikes *Macs* ever since she got the flu and the smell of a *Big Mac* made her feel sicker.

After their burgers, they drove around, then stopped at a mini-mall and Farren says," I'll be back in a minute Ellen, ok?"

"I'll be here. Is it ok to listen to the radio?" she asked, wondering what he was up to.

"Just turn the key backwards Ellen and it will come back on, I'll be right back."

"Ok Farren, thank you."

About ten minutes later he was back with a shopping bag in his hand. With a big grin on his face, he holds up the bag, opens Ellen's door and places it on her lap saying, "For you Madame."

Ellen's cheeks were flushed and hot as she struggled for the right words to come out of her mouth. She attempted to thank him for his thoughtfulness.

Then just like Scarlet O'Hara she says, "Why Farren, you didn't have to get me anything, I don't have anything to give you. Thank you Farren, no one has ever given me a gift before, as a boyfriend I mean."

"Well you better check it out before you thank me, it's really not that much. Your welcome Ellen, now have a look." as he leaned towards Ellen and kissed her cheek.

As she opened up the bag she didn't know what to expect. Then she realized he had gotten her the yellow floppy plastic sun hat with gold dots on it, the gold chain belt and sun glasses that she had wanted so bad.

"How did you know, Farren? I wanted these, like forever; thank you so much," as she gave him a big hug.

"You're so welcome Ellen; Deanna and Helena had them put away for me. They knew you wanted them, so I thought it would a nice surprise for you, seeing as I wasn't around on your last birthday. I really like you, Ellen. I hope we can see a lot more of each other," he said as he gave Ellen a hug and kissed her forehead.

"I'll treasure my gifts always, Farren." she said overwhelmed by his kindness and so happy to be with him that evening.

"You're so sweet Ellen, I'm glad you like your gift. Now we better get a move on—we have time to catch a movie at the drive-in; how about it, want to go?"

"I love the drive-in Farren, I'd love to go." she said bubbling over with the thought of cuddling next to Farren at the Drive-in.

That night at the Drive-in, parked in the front row, the evening was everything Ellen could have hoped for. Farren was a perfect gentleman, the movie was great and she did cuddle up while they watched the show. At intermission while she went to the washroom Farren went to the canteen, bringing back a large buttery popcorn and pop for them to munch on.

He placed the popcorn between them and looked over at her and says, "I can't believe how beautiful you are Ellen." cupping her face in his hands and kissed her gently.

He was such a gentle person, that she responded to that kiss and kissed him back, "I really like you Farren, you're very sweet." she whispered, hoping she wasn't sounding corny.

Intermission was over so Farren put his arm around Ellen and the movie was good. But Ellen was so comfortable in his arms, she fell asleep. He let her sleep through the rest of the show. She didn't awake until they were nearly back to her house.

When she realized she had slept through most of the evening she was so embarrassed she didn't know what to say except, "I'm so sorry Farren, I feel like an idiot."

"You're not an idiot, silly girl; I enjoyed having a pretty girl on my shoulder." He laughed as he brushed Ellen's hair out of her eyes.

"Now let's get you home young lady, you need your beauty sleep," as he turned down Ellen's road.

"I really enjoyed myself Farren, even though I missed half the night, thank you for being so sweet."

It was funny but yet so sweet of him to let her sleep and not make her uncomfortable about it.

"Goodnight Ellen. Can I see you next Saturday about eight?"

Ellen didn't hesitate as she said, "Sure Farren, I can't wait, thank you for everything."

She ran to the house and when her head hit the pillow she was so happy she drifted off to sleep in no time.

But there wasn't to be another night with Farren thanks to his older brother Blaine, whom she met briefly at Farren's house but didn't take much notice of.

19: Why did he not keep their date?

She sat anxiously by her bedroom window, waiting and wondering why Farren hadn't called to say he'd be late or some explanation. It wasn't because she didn't want to see Farren that Saturday.

Finally, a car pulls up in the front yard but it wasn't Farren—it was Blaine, Farren's brother.

Thinking something must have happened, she ran out to see what was going on.

"Hi Blaine, is Farren alright? Where is he? He was supposed to pick me up at eight," not having a clue what he was about to tell her.

"Well Ellen, I don't know how to tell you this but Farren sent me to tell you, he had a date with his ex-girlfriend. They are getting back together. He said to tell you he is sorry and hopes you'll understand."

He was so sympathetic, and understanding, she believed he was telling her the truth.

Devastated and sobbing, "Thank you Blaine, but you can tell your brother I don't understand him or forgive him, and never to talk to me again."

"I will, Ellen. I'm so sorry, can I make it up to you? We could go for a drive, get a burger or whatever you want."

Ellen almost felt like accepting his offer but she refused.

"Your very kind Blaine, but I just want to be alone right now, but thank you for asking. Good night Blaine, thank you again for your trouble."

"It's no trouble Ellen, I feel terrible for all this. It feels almost like it's my fault. Maybe you would reconsider another night?"

He said this in such a soft, reassuring tone that had Ellen totally confused.

"Why would you think this would be your fault Blaine? Don't be silly, Farren makes his own decisions doesn't he? Ellen did not know how ironic the situation really was.

"Well, I just feel responsible for my little brother's inconsideration. You deserve so much better Ellen. Will you please, maybe let me make it up to you?"

He was still trying to get her to go with him. But for some reason Ellen didn't want to have anything to do with this guy. She couldn't figure out why she felt that way.

"No, I really want to just go to my room and be alone. Alright Blaine? Good night and thank you again." Hoping he would just take the hint and leave.

"Ok Ellen, I'll call you. I hope you will be ok, goodnight."

He was still assuming he could replace Farren or something, Ellen thought it all seemed kind of freaky.

Well, Ellen accepted the fact that obviously Farren had changed his mind about her. But it really hurt the way he did it, not telling her face to face or at least by a phone call. That night she cried, and cried some more until her tears all dried up.

Ellen said her prayers that night and stayed in her room alone, not telling anyone what had happened except her best friend;

Dear Lord,

I guess You already know what happened with Farren. Dear Lord, I was hoping You could help me understand and accept it. I thought Farren really liked me and we were going to see a lot of each other. I was so happy with him. I guess I will just wait and see what I'm supposed to do next and spend some time with Andrea and stuff. Show me what to do Lord.

Amen

Thank you

Love Ellen

Life takes so many different turns. Circumstances have a way of changing over night for no apparent reason. Ellen was not leading her direction—the Lord was. Continuously leading, teaching and preparing her for the future. Whether the road ahead was rough or smooth, she had to learn how to make decisions and face the consequences. She always prayed *He* had a direction and a plan for her future. Although she may not have found it yet, she will. Ellen will continue to learn, write and pray.

Ellen's prayer is that her story, her life will find its way to anyone that might find any source of comfort, direction, or an understanding. We are not alone in this life no matter how old, or who we are. *He* is always close by, *EVEN NOW, YOU LEAD ME*; never forget this. So seek that comfort and you'll never be alone no matter what this life holds. *He* will never leave us.

20: After Farren

The next day the phone was ringing, waking Ellen up from a sound sleep.

It was Helena and she was all excited about something, "Ellen, Ellen are you totally awake? I want to come over. I just got to show you my new boots. Mom got me the cutest scooter skirt and top, and got you almost the same set. Kind of like two for one, you know?"

"Well, sounds like I'll be seeing you soon." Helena was just like a sister.

Helena laughed "I'll be there in time for breakfast. Tell your Mom. You're just going to love this outfit Ellen, love you, bye."

'Well, thought Ellen, 'I guess Helena is the answer to my prayer. 'Enjoy my friends, my family, and my life.' 'I'm only fifteen; I have lots of time for the serious things in life.'

Ellen's decision to just enjoy being fifteen was almost a relief—relief from the pressure and the fear of the expectation of having a bad relationship. She looked forward to sleepovers with Helena and Deanna. They were free to do the things young girls love; dancing, telling stories, pillow fights and late lunches served by their Moms.

Andrea happily kept Ellen company—she loved having her big sister around. They enjoyed many a night that summer hanging out with their cousins.

21: Ellen's First Funeral

In Ellen's last year of high school there was a young man named Dougie who was on the honour roll. Everyone loved him, he excelled in everything. He was handsome, had earned a scholarship, and had his own little Volkswagen Beetle which he drove back and forth to High School. He was a teenage dream and had it all as far as everyone was concerned. All the girls were gaga over Dougie. He was just so busy with being the President of the Student Council, soccer, and every other activity he was involved in, and then there were his studies. That wouldn't give him much time for a social life, would it?

Ellen didn't know Dougie very well, but when Clarice, (Ellen's cousin) called her about two weeks before graduation she was devastated. Apparently Dougie had been on his way home from a practice when, on a sharp turn just before his home, a drunk driver hit him head on and killed him instantly. It was terrible—a young man with his whole life ahead, gone in a matter of seconds. Clarice was calling to ask if Ellen would go to the funeral with her, since most everyone in the high school was going out of respect for Dougie.

"I have never been to a funeral before Clarice. I don't know how I would handle it. But seeing Dougie was such a special person, I'll go with you."

"Great Ellen, I really didn't want to go by myself. Why don't you come stay with me tonight, and you can get ready here?"

"How would I get to your place?"

"Mom would be happy to come get you."

"Ok, Dougie was such a great guy. Everyone respected him. He had everything going for him. It's just too sad."

"We'll be over in a little bit. You get ready Ellen."

"I will Clarice, and thank you for asking me. I'll be ready."

Ellen threw a couple of her favourite outfits, shoes, and a few other things in her bag. She heard the horn blowing. "Clarice is here, Mom. See you when I get back. Love you Mom."

"Alright sweetheart. I love you. Say hi to Clarice and tell that sister of mine to call me." as she blew Ellen a kiss.

22: Dougie's Wake

That evening at the wake, it was unbelievable the number of people that passed through the church paying their respects to Dougie and his family.

Ellen had never dreamed how Dougie would look lying in a casket. His face was cold and expressionless. His eyes permanently closed, never to see the wonders of this world. His hands were folded, never to play his favourite sports. His hair motionless, never to be tossed aside by the wind. His body still, never to run, play or love again.

But he looked at peace. The peace Ellen saw on his face gave her the feeling that God already had taken Dougie to be with him. From that moment on she felt she would not fear death—and she doesn't. She feels sadness at the loss of a loved one, yet at peace, knowing they have simply gone before us and will watch over us all until we go home.

From that day on Ellen looked at her life and the lives of her family and friends differently. Life everlasting became more real to her. She wanted to lead a life that would reflect that knowledge. Although we are only human, we are made in His image and she wanted—and still wants—to live up to that image. Sure she forgets at times that she cannot carry on her shoulders the burdens of all she loves. But when that weight gets so heavy she soon remembers *Who* to turn to.

The next day's funeral was equally moving. More aware of her surroundings, she heard the birds chirping in the trees all around the cemetery, saw the perfect flowers at most of the grave sides and the blue sky above all, highlighting the obvious love on the faces of the many people that attended Dougie's funeral.

Ellen reflects, 'When I awake some quiet, clear mornings to the sounds of the birds chirping, the gentle breeze rustling the leaves and see the blue sky through the window, it brings me back to the day we said, *'Farewell for now,'* to a young man I hadn't even spoken a word to. Yet I felt connected to him and will never forget his image to this day.'

We will all have many losses and experiences in our lives, but it is how we look at them that will get us through. Ellen has learned to lean on *God* to help her through. *He* always does, even when she gets stubborn and tries to handle it on her own. "I just can't handle anything without Him and I know that."

23: Ellen Meets Terry

When Ellen first met the young man who was to become her husband, she was in love at first sight. It was a quiet evening—May 10th 1971 to be exact....

She hadn't been in a relationship for a while and was having fun hanging out with Andrea. They danced, sewed, made hand-drawn colouring books, and talked to their cousins on the phone.

Ellen had been in her room making birch bark canoes for her cousins when she heard a car pull into their yard. Mom and Dad were downstairs, so she looked out her bedroom window to see if she could catch a glimpse of who it was. She could only see the tops of two heads, and remembers they were wearing tams or toques.

Curiosity got the best of her, so downstairs she trotted, trying to be all cool and everything as she went to the kitchen wood stove and leaned on the warming oven. All the while, she was trying to catch a glimpse of who were under those tams.

It was two cute guys, one with golden brown wavy hair and blue eyes and the other with jet black hair—she never took notice of the colour of the second one's eyes. The one with the golden brown hair was saying to Dad that he was celebrating his birthday and wanted to hear him play the fiddle.

Ellen was clueless who these guys were, but she felt drawn to this guy with the mass of golden brown hair under that old tam. His eyes were the clearest crystal blue she had ever seen. When he glanced over at Ellen and smiled, her feet nearly went out from under her.

She noticed he had taken a cigarette out of his white t-shirt pocket and he didn't have a light for it. So this is how the rest of Ellen's life began....

She nervously reached for the box of matches from the warming oven, took one of the wooden matches out, walked over to this total stranger, and said, "Would you like a light?"

He looked up at Ellen with those piercing blue eyes, "Thank you." As he put the cigarette to his lips, Ellen struck the match and held it to the cigarette. He took a breath in to ignite it, and

Even Now You Lead Me

then exhaled, turning his head away so as not to blow smoke in her face. So began a union of their hearts to this day.

Ellen held out her hand to introduce herself, "Hi, I'm Ellen."

He then took Ellen's hand, shook it and introduced himself, "Hi I'm Terry and that's my friend Jamie. Today is my 20th birthday. Jamie and I want to hear some of your dad's tunes. So nice to meet you, Ellen."

"It's nice to meet you Terry, and you too Jamie," as she walked back to the stove and listened for a few more minutes.

She felt out of place, so she excused herself and went back upstairs to her room.

24: Ellen's Letter and Prayer

In those days there were no computers, so communication was either by phone or pen & paper. Her cousin Helena must be informed about her meeting Terry. So she began to write....

Dear Helena:

Hey girl, I just had to write to you before I fall asleep. I met the cutest guy this evening; his name is Terry. He wanted to hear Dad play the fiddle for his birthday. He is so cute, he's got gorgeous blue eyes, sandy brown hair, and about 5ft. 9 or so. He's got a sweet smile and wears a tam. I think he might be a fisherman; anyway he is gorgeous and I pray he will come back to see me. I lit his cigarette and he looked up at me with those blue eyes and said thank you. I know I sound silly, Helena, but I feel like I already know him or something. I told him my name and he said his name was Terry and introduced me to his friend Jamie. Then I went and stood back at the stove for a little while and then I came up to my room. They were listening to Dad anyway. You know I don't like the fiddle. But I really hope he comes back. He is really cute, Helena, and he seems like a nice guy. He seems to know Dad really well, don't know how yet. I wonder if he liked me? Oh, I better stop. Say a prayer for me, and so will I. Goodnight, Helena, love you.

Love, Ellen

PS, make sure you write back or come see me if you can. Love you, girl.

She put Helena's letter in an envelope hoping Mom would have a stamp so she could run out and put it in the mailbox in the morning. Lying back on her pillow, she thought of how she was going to pray that *God* would bring Terry back to her—it went like this:

Dear Lord,

Hi, God, you know today I met a cute guy, his name is Terry. He was with his friend Jamie. Terry is really nice and so cute. Could You bring him back to see me? I think

Even Now You Lead Me

he is going to be really nice to me, and he has really blue eyes. I really like him Lord. If I promise to be good and you bring him back, I will be very grateful, and I will never forget to pray. Take care of my family, Lord, and please help my Dad stay sober, be nice to Mom and not do bad things. Thank You.

I love You, God,

Love Ellen

25: Reflections

When Ellen reflects back to her teen years, she finds it so hard to space the time....

Back then it seemed a month was a whole year, and now a year passes as a day. Time now flies by, faster each year. Looking back, she used to think she and each of her ex-boyfriends were in a relationship for a long time, but actually four or five evenings were all they shared.

From the time of her first date at fifteen until she met the man she was destined to marry, there was one bad relationship; one that made her feel second best; one that she thought would be *the* one; and three that turned out to be just a pleasant drive with friends.

Being a girl from the country, she found the simple things in life made her happy. She was content with a drive on a lovely evening with her best friends, going to the beach, or a quiet night at the drive-in. She loved going dancing with cousins whether they had dates or not. They enjoyed each other's company. In our modern age, dating no longer seems to include doing things, as they once enjoyed.

Abandoned farmhouses, still hold fascination for Ellen and her sister's to this day. Although they rarely get to go on adventures as they once did, they now enjoy taking pictures of the remains of old buildings. She stops and captures the past through the windows of one room schoolhouses, and the many different churches on her Island. She also takes pleasure in photos she takes of sunrise, sunset, and the moon.

To this day Ellen always avoids house parties. Too often a night out with friends involves going to a bar, a lot of drinking and usually ending in a brawl. Today's lifestyles are so fast-paced there is no time to enjoy relaxing and getting to know one another.

People in relationships don't want to work at it and tend to give up on one another too easily—just move on to greener pastures. No one is perfect and all have to go through many ups and downs in their life. But if you don't *work* at a relationship, then you have no hope of a future with anyone.

26: Conclusion Stories

Ellen's Dad (Donald). The last few years of his life were his best—he quit drinking, and became a good dad and granddad as well. After he had suffered a couple of heart attacks, their Dad and Mom decided they would both quit smoking.

Her mother had smoked in secret for a while—Ellen didn't know how long, but she knew for some time and kept it to herself. Her mother just up and said to her father one day "If you can smoke so can I." And she did.

Then their Dad went for open heart surgery in 2001 promising Ellen to bring her a feed of mackerel when he got home, but he never made it. He suffered a stroke on the table and went into a coma.

He was on life support, and the family was called to make the trip across the big bridge to the hospital in N.B. The family arrived at the hospital to say their goodbyes. They were all there for him, and Ellen hoped he could feel the forgiveness in the room and the love they had for him. She told Dad that she and her husband were there to see him. He opened his eyes briefly and gave them a smile—she then knew that he knew all was forgiven.

The family was faced with the agonizing decision to end life support that day. Ellen heard her sisters Joyce and Andrea say, "Whatever was done is done and all is forgiven, Dad."

Leroy was so upset; his Dad was his best friend. Ellen remembers him just lying back on the hotel bed with his hands over his eyes. The girls stayed with their Mom that night in a hotel room, waiting with her until word came. Their Dad left them the day before their Mom's birthday on Nov 9th, 2001. Doreen stayed by her husbands side up until they stopped life support, she could not bare to stay.

(Doreen) Mom. Their mom, Doreen, is a petite little ninety-eight pound, four-foot-eight lady, who is adored by all who know her. She is only seventeen years older than Ellen and is such a pretty little lady. She loves sewing, dancing, hanging out with her friends and her surviving six sisters. After her husband Donald passed away, Doreen learned to drive and got her license.

She became a very independent lady, and was more or less happy, to feel she was free to go and do, as she wanted. Doreen through all her years of marriage to Donald, depended on him to take her wherever they needed to go. Shopping was somewhat supervised and on a time schedule as he was untrusting of her. She faithfully stayed by his side despite all his shortcomings.

She was always a quiet woman as far as sharing her life stories with her children. With her children all grown, with families of their own, she still wasn't completely ready to share how her childhood or married life struggles were, with them. But with Ellen's inquisitive nature, the last few years have begun to bring Doreen out of the shell she seemed to keep herself in.

Doreen was a child in The Depression Years. She and her eight sisters and three brothers learned how to make do with what you were given. Their play was outdoors most of the time, their meals came from their own crops, neighbouring farmers and a local store, perhaps in a family members home. Times were hard and neighbours helped each other all year round.

Ellen delights in her Moms stories of school years when Doreen was the girl chosen to draw Santa Claus and Christmas trees on the chalk board. The Halloween pranks they would carry out on their father and his neighbour, who seemed to have an ongoing feud, and the sleigh ride adventures with her sisters and a boy from the farm down the road, were like fantasy adventures for Ellen.

But as with Ellen and her sisters, there was an ere of secrecy throughout their lives, that no one spoke of.

Just last year Doreen lost the man she fell in love for the past nine years to cancer. Doreen was so in love with him, they did everything together. Yet he new a woman needs a measure of freedom and he gave her what she needed if she wanted to do errands or anything on her own.

Ellen mentioned she was a bit jealous of her mother for having a man that actually danced with her and beautifully as well. On the dance floor all eyes were on them as they swayed across the floor. Ellen fondly called him Bo Dad, she smiles as she thinks back on them on the dance floor. Bo Dad would have one arm

Even Now You Lead Me

around Doreen's waist and the other behind his back, smiling, and looking into the eyes of his adoring young love.

All Ellen's family thought the world of Bo, and are forever thankful for the time they shared together.

Ellen proudly says, "It was easy to call him *Dad.* He treated Mom like gold, and she so deserved the royal treatment. They were like a couple of teenagers in love, so sweet."

Ellen only wishes that they would of had more time to have spent together, but the time her Mom had with Bo was so well spent.

She is still a very independent woman to this day, living in her own home with the ongoing help from her children and their families. She is busy with her sewing for the neighborhood, friends and family. Then she is a pro at preserves of any kind, and bread and biscuits are as they say, *To Die For.*

(Leroy) little brother. Leroy took the death of his father very hard. They had been best buddies. They'd worked together, fixing old vehicles in their garage, and were both musicians, full of music to the end.

Leroy was the kind of man who was everyone's big brother. He'd do anything he possibly could for anyone. He adored his twin girls, Kathy and Katie, and they loved their Dad dearly. His last evening, he was tucking his precious girls in for the night when he suffered a terrible heart attack.

Leroy played in a Rock Band as well, with Andrea, her husband James, and James's brother Tony. Ellen still listens to his cassette tape and sings along to the songs that he and her sister Andrea composed together. The song's they wrote and recorded will always hold a place in the heart of every family member. One song that Leroy wrote, and put the music to, was for one of his girls who was in the hospital and the nurses that cared for her. It was called 'Here's to the Girls in Unit Five, from a Big Tuff Daddy That Almost Cried.'

No doubt those nurses cried for sure after they heard this touching thank you from Leroy.

Leaving his family just three months after their Dad, was a terrible shock to the whole family. Kathy and Katie adored their Dad, but Ellen and her family were unsure of Leroy's wife's feeling for him, for she remarried a man from away just five months after his passing. Leroy was just forty-five years of age.

Ellen says she feels her Dad and her brother, aren't really far away at all, just around the corner.

Ellen's best Friend—sister Andrea. Ellen's sister, Andrea, is four years younger and has always been her best friend...

Andrea became Ellen's protection from harm and most likely the same could be said for Andrea. Together they were safe. Their closeness has helped both girls deal with life and their faith has made them whole, giving them the ability to share their love and their lives with their own families. They are like two peas in a pod and have always shared their lives—the good and the bad—kind of like a twin connection. Sometimes though, Andrea still finds it hard to totally let burdens go and share them with Ellen. But when she does, they usually can give them to God and find peace.

To this day Ellen and Andrea share so many of life's trials and happy times as well. Together they have done their best to bring their family members to the knowledge of Jesus and what He has and will do for us. Andreas second husband James and Ellen's Terry have gone through good and bad times. Terry has struggled with addictions over the years and like her mother, Ellen stuck by him.

James has always considered Terry his best friend and through the years has prayed faithfully for his friend to find and accept Jesus into his heart. The faithful prayers of Ellen, Andrea and James are being answered. Terry now attends church with them and has joined a small group at their church.

Terry confessed that he never felt he was worthy of God's love, and was overwhelmed when his new friends and old put their hands on his and Ellen's shoulders and prayed that God would enter into his life and take away his constant ailments.

Both Terry and Ellen have told their friends that they feel a huge burden has been lifted from them.

(Joyce) Poetic Sister. Although Joyce and her family have moved away to Ontario, they all keep in touch by mail, phone, and now computer. She and her family packed up and left their Island home to get their children's lives on a better track.

Her children are all adults now and she still prays and does everything she can to help them keep their lives in order. Joyce is now a grandmother and is presently raising one her grandsons, and helps with the care of three of her other daughter's children.

Only over the last few years have Joyce and Ellen developed a real close relationship. Joyce is a wonderfully gifted writer of God's word. She has rolled out beautiful pieces every few days over the years, each one more powerful than the one before.

Through these masterpieces Ellen has come to learn much about Joyce—especially as she describes her troubles and experiences as a child. Her writing reveals that all three older sisters were alone with their inner secrets and could not tell anyone but God.

Joyce is very much still an Islander at heart and she and her husband take advantage of holidays to come home for a visit to her family.

Joyce and her husband Roy plan to retire home on the Island on their Mom's property so they can care for her if need be.

Joyce is presently working on getting her GEDs and a diploma.

(Melinda) Baby Sister. Last but not least, with a temper and attitude to go with her flaming red hair, came baby sister Melinda.

Ellen thinking back, 'I'm afraid she was spoiled; she was so cute—even when she was having one of her little tantrums.'

Melinda needed a lot of attention and assurance of their love. Being thirteen years older, Ellen guessed she served more as a second Mom to her then a big sister—something she always considered special.

If she loved you, Melinda was the kind of girl that loved you to death—but get on her wrong side then watch out! She may have grown to four foot ten or so but she can sure still hold her ground and has done so many times.

With the loss of her father and brother so close together, Melinda particularly found the loss hard to take. She felt that she alone bore the weight of their deaths and became very untrusting of most people.

Being Mom's baby, she still checks in every day with a phone call, just to make sure Mom is fine.

Melinda's marriage of nineteen years to Stephen was blessed with a beautiful daughter, Stephanie. They tried many times to have another child after Stephanie, but each time she conceived it was a difficult, tubal pregnancy. This left her with little hope of having another child without life-threatening complications.

After divorcing, Stephen and Melinda both remarried, but neither of their new marriages lasted, either. Melinda distanced herself from her family for a while, but then she met another young man - Kenny. He has proven to be more compatible—most of the time. She seems to have found her place in life.

Lately her phone calls to Ellen have become more frequent, as she often reminds Ellen how much she loves her big sister.

Suzie Doll. Ellen's favourite companion next to Andrea was her Suzie doll, given to Ellen for Christmas by her first Grade teacher, Mary Ross. It was a gift she treasured all her life. She often wished Suzie could talk as she made her new outfits, told her secrets, held her in her arms, put her to sleep, then tucked her into her little bed she made out of a box, complete with a pillow, and blankets.

Maybe Ellen felt she was destined to be a doctor—she performed an eye transplant by transferring Suzie's blue eyes to her Tommy doll, and Tommy's brown eyes became Suzie's. The eye operation was a success and brown-eyed Suzie to this day is still in the family.

But she will always have the scars, stitches on the corners of her mouth thanks to little brother Leroy and his bright idea of opening her mouth.

Even Now You Lead Me

Ellen's granddaughter Krista now has Suzie and takes very good care of her. She gave Suzie to Krista for her first birthday, and Krista's Mommy, (Ellen's oldest daughter Lorraine) cared for Suzie until Krista could take over. Suzie is a story in herself.

27: New Beginnings

Guess what—Terry came back three days later. Ellen was so bubbly and excited; she had to shake herself to calm down enough to ask Mom if she could go for a drive with Terry and his friend. Mom said she could go. So began Ellen's life with the man of her dreams.

By the way, Terry and Ellen married five and a half months after they met. Life since then has not all been a bouquet of roses. She has survived and grown from mistakes and good and bad experiences. Through it all *God* has been by her side.

Ellen concludes: I have come to believe that I am here to help others, through understanding my own life and sharing it with you all. We all need true friends and someone to turn to. We don't need to feel we are alone. My hopes are that you would teach your children to come to you if they are afraid or don't understand something in their young lives.

We are their protection from harm and with the *Lord's* guidance we will find our way. Children should never be allowed to go unsupervised with someone, if there is the slightest chance that the person might be a risk to the child.

Our children should be made aware; if they're not comfortable in any way with someone, to go to someone they trust and tell them. If my experiences can prevent other children from being taken advantage of in any way, I'll be very thankful.

I feel I have a responsibility to tell you that these bad things happen very close to home and our children have to be protected, and us parents have to be watchful of our children and teens as well.

Ellen's Advice. I tell my story with the hope of encouraging parents, children and teens that if you experience anything similar to what my sisters and I have experienced, don't be ashamed, *it's not your fault*. Please don't be afraid to go to someone you trust and tell them what is happening to you. *Don't keep it a secret* as we felt we had to.

With this I think I will close. May I just add if anyone finds Ellen's story helpful and would like to hear how Ellen's new relationship with Terry evolved, I would be happy to share those adventures. It is Ellen's wish that all children will be given the chance to have a good life and come to know the awesome *Love of our Lord and Saviour.*

www.ingramcontent.com/pod-product-compliance
Lightning Source LLC
Chambersburg PA
CBHW050043080526
44586CB00014B/1429